World's WEIRDEST Animals
Thorny Devils

Big Buddy Books
An Imprint of Abdo Publishing
abdopublishing.com

Marcia Zappa

abdopublishing.com

Published by Abdo Publishing, a division of ABDO, PO Box 398166, Minneapolis, Minnesota 55439. Copyright © 2016 by Abdo Consulting Group, Inc. International copyrights reserved in all countries. No part of this book may be reproduced in any form without written permission from the publisher. Big Buddy Books™ is a trademark and logo of Abdo Publishing.

Printed in the United States of America, North Mankato, Minnesota.
042015
092015

THIS BOOK CONTAINS
RECYCLED MATERIALS

Cover Photos: Peter Walton Photography/Getty Images; Shutterstock.com.
Interior Photos: ©Densey Clyne/AUSCAPE (p. 23); ©Gerry Ellis/Minden Pictures (p. 25); ©Michael & Patricia Fogden/Minden Pictures (p. 15); ©Paul A. Souders/CORBIS/Glow Images (p. 7); Ann & Steve Toon/Glow Images (p. 11); ©Greg Harold/AUSCAPE/Glow Images (p. 27); ©iStockphoto.com (pp. 9, 21); ©Mitsuaki Iwago/Minden Pictures (p. 17); KonArt/Deposit Photos (pp. 5, 29); Shutterstock.com (pp. 19, 30).

Coordinating Series Editor: Rochelle Baltzer
Contributing Editors: Megan M. Gunderson, Bridget O'Brien, Sarah Tieck
Graphic Design: Adam Craven

Library of Congress Cataloging-in-Publication Data

Zappa, Marcia, 1985- author.
  Thorny devils / Marcia Zappa.
      pages cm. -- (World's weirdest animals)
  ISBN 978-1-62403-779-5
1. Agamidae--Juvenile literature. 2. Lizards--Australia--Juvenile literature. 3. Adaptation (Biology)--Juvenile literature. I. Title.
  QL666.L223Z37 2016
  597.95'5--dc23
                                  2015005565

Contents

Wildly Weird!

The world is full of weird, wonderful animals. Thorny devils are almost entirely covered in pointy spines. These small lizards live in Australia.

Thorny devils have several unusual talents. They can change color, puff themselves up, and drink water off their bodies. All of these features make thorny devils wildly weird!

Thorny devils are also called thorny dragons, thorny lizards, and mountain devils.

Bold Bodies

Thorny devils are lizards. Lizards are reptiles, which are cold-blooded animals covered in scales.

A thorny devil's scales have sharp spines. Almost all of the spines are made of strong matter called keratin.

Did You Know?

Human fingernails are also made of keratin.

A thorny devil's spines may look strange. But, they help it survive.

A thorny devil has a flattened body, short legs, and a tail that often sticks up. It has a small head and pointed face.

Thorny devils grow up to 8 inches (20 cm) long. They weigh up to 3.1 ounces (89 g).

LEG

BODY

HEAD

EYE

TAIL

9

Colorful Creatures

Thorny devils change color. This helps them blend into their **habitat** and stay safe from **predators**. They may change based on temperature or time of day. Thorny devils can be yellow, olive green, reddish, or brown.

Thorny devils are known to change color quickly when scared.

Where in the World?

Thorny devils live in central and western Australia. They are found in sandy deserts and dry scrublands. They hide under spiky grasses and acacia shrubs.

Did You Know?

Thorny devils are similar to North America's horned lizards. They share traits such as spines, which help them survive. But, they are not related.

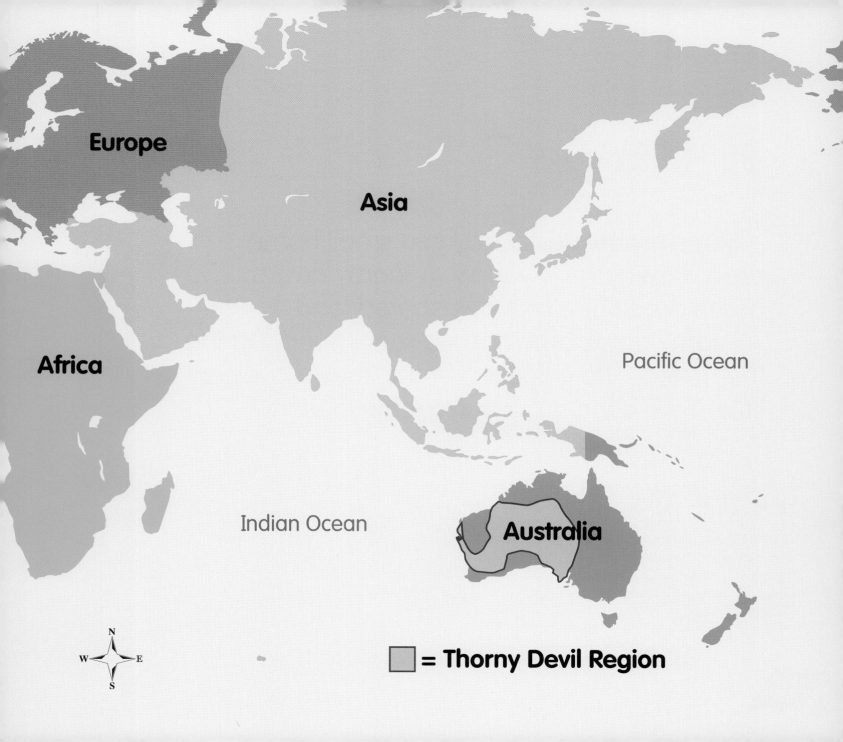

Europe

Asia

Africa

Pacific Ocean

Indian Ocean

Australia

N
W   E
S

■ = **Thorny Devil Region**

A Devil's Life

Some thorny devils stay in a small home area. Others travel widely. A thorny devil's home area often includes shared land.

Thorny devils aren't active year-round. During the hottest and coldest months, they move very little. They each dig a **burrow** for shelter.

Did You Know?

Australia's seasons are opposite of North America's. So, a thorny devil's hottest months are January and February. Its coldest months are June and July.

Like other reptiles, thorny devils are cold-blooded. Their body heat comes from outside. So, they spend time sunning themselves.

Thorny devils are known for their slow walk. They rock backward and forward. And, they often freeze in place.

Thorny devils have many **predators**. Humans, lizards, and birds hunt them. Wild dogs called dingoes are also a threat.

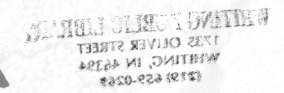

A thorny devil's unusual walk makes it hard to spot. This keeps it safe from predators.

Safety First

A thorny devil's many sharp spines are enough to keep most **predators** away. But, this lizard has other ways to stay safe as well.

A thorny devil has a round lump on the back of its neck. It is known as a false head. And, a thorny devil puffs itself up by filling its chest with air. Both features make the animal hard to handle or swallow.

When scared, a thorny devil can tuck its real head between its legs. Then, the false head looks like its real head. This keeps its real head safe.

19

Ant Eater

Thorny devils eat black ants. They must eat a lot of these small insects to **survive**. In fact, some scientists believe thorny devils eat thousands of ants every day!

Scientists say thorny devils are obligate myrmecophages (AH-blih-guht muhr-muh-KAHF-uh-guhs). This fancy phrase means they only eat ants.

Thorny devils are made to eat ants. Their sticky tongues help them grab the small insects. And, they have special teeth to cut the hard outer body of an ant.

Thorny devils are **patient** hunters. They find ant trails. Then, they simply wait for their **prey** to pass by.

Did You Know?

Thorny devil droppings break apart easily. This reveals all the hard outer shells from the ants they eat.

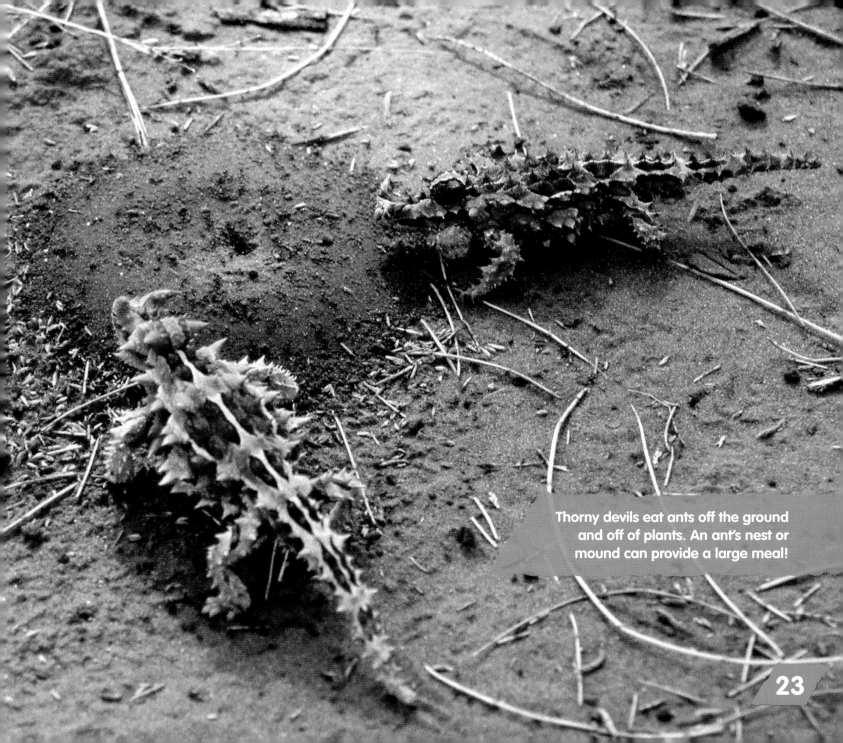

Thorny devils eat ants off the ground and off of plants. An ant's nest or mound can provide a large meal!

Thirst-Quenching Spines

A thorny devil has a weird way of getting a drink. Its spines help it get water. Between its spines are small **grooves**. Water from dew and rain collects in these. Then, the water flows to a thorny devil's mouth so it can drink.

Much of the water a thorny devil drinks comes from dew that collects on its body. This is often the best way to get water on the dry land it calls home.

Life Cycle

Thorny devils usually **mate** between late winter and early summer. Then, a mother digs a special **burrow**. She lays three to ten eggs in it.

After 90 to 132 days, the eggs **hatch**. Babies are small. They eat their own eggshells to gain weight and strength. Then, they climb out of the burrow and begin eating ants.

Did You Know?

After laying eggs, a mother thorny devil leaves the burrow and closes the entrance. This helps keep the eggs hidden.

Newly hatched thorny devils usually weigh less than 0.07 ounces (2 g). They begin growing right away.

World Wide Weird

Thorny devils are common in their territory. Few people live in the middle of Australia. But there are some roads, and thorny devils like to warm themselves there. So, drivers must watch for them.

It is important to know how our actions affect wild animals. With care, we can keep weird, wonderful animals such as thorny devils around for years to come.

Did You Know?
The thorny devil's interesting appearance makes it popular in zoos.

Thorny devils live up to 20 years!

FAST FACTS ABOUT:
Thorny Devils

Animal Type – reptile

Size – up to 8 inches (20 cm) long

Weight – up to about 3.1 ounces (89 g)

Habitat – sandy deserts and dry scrublands in central and western Australia

Diet – ants

What makes the thorny devil wildly weird?
It is covered in spines, it has a fake head, it changes color, and it gets its drinking water off its own body!

Glossary

burrow an animal's underground home.

groove a long, narrow channel cut into something.

habitat a place where a living thing is naturally found.

hatch to be born from an egg.

mate to join as a couple in order to reproduce, or have babies.

patient (PAY-shehnt) not hasty or reckless.

predator a person or animal that hunts and kills animals for food.

prey an animal hunted or killed by a predator for food.

survive to continue to live or exist.

Websites

To learn more about World's Weirdest Animals, visit **booklinks.abdopublishing.com**. These links are routinely monitored and updated to provide the most current information available.

31

Index

WHITING PUBLIC LIBRARY
1735 OLIVER STREET
WHITING, IN 46394
(219) 659-0269